Suggestions for th[...]
and others concerned wi[...]

GW01466554

WORKING
TOGETHER

Barbara Cockburn
Alec Ross

Teaching in Higher Education Series
ISSN 0309-3565

No.3: Working Together
ISBN 0-90169950-0
   School of Education, University of Lancaster

Published by School of Education, University of Lancaster,
Bailrigg, Lancaster, LA1 4YL, England.

Printed in England by Titus Wilson, Kendal.

FOREWORD

This booklet is one of a series produced with the aid of
a grant from the University Grants Committee as part of
its programme for the development of knowledge about and
skill in teaching in higher education. The series is
intended to bring together traditional wisdom (not a
source to be neglected) research findings when available
and relevant, and summaries of what is regarded by the
informed as good practice.

The sub-title "Suggestions for the consideration of
those concerned ..." echoes that of a famous manual for
the guidance of elementary school teachers and this
series shares the same purpose. The handbooks may at
times be mildly hortatory but they are not meant to be
prescriptive. Teaching is something of an art and the
aim is to encourage, within sensible limits, something
of a personal style. The "rules" (if such they be)
are constantly broken by successful teachers but few,
if any, get away with breaking all the rules all the
time.

Universities and other institutions of higher education
have traditionally accepted research and teaching as
their principal functions. The systems developed for
training in research are well worked out. Till now
little has been done for teaching. The initiative
taken by the University Grants Committee was widely
welcomed and has led to an increasing awareness in
higher education generally of the importance of giving
to the teaching function the attention it deserves.
This series is intended to offer help to those who wish
to make an effort to improve their teaching. It is
hoped that those who read these pages will, as a result,
be better prepared for this important aspect of their
daily work.

The authors would be glad to receive reports and
illustrative material which readers may wish to send
with a view to improving the next edition of these
booklets.

C.F. CARTER
Vice-Chancellor
University of Lancaster.

PREFACE TO THE FOUR BOOKLETS ON SMALL GROUP TEACHING

WORKING TOGETHER   PARTICIPATORY DISCUSSION
A KIND OF LEARNING   PATTERNS AND PROCEDURES

Seminars and tutorials, though sometimes formally defined,
embrace a wide range of activities; choices must be made.
These booklets are to introduce the new tutor to the
strengths and weaknesses of the small group and to ways
of organising it for different purposes.   We describe:

Group behaviour.
This is the main part of "Working Together".

Strategies for making group work more effective.
These are the strategies for improving a group's working
together (in "Working Together") and strategies for
achieving different intellectual objectives, set out in
"Patterns and Procedures" and "A Kind of Learning".

Tactics small group tutors can use.
Group management and discussion skills are described in
"Working Together" and "Participatory Discussion".   The
organisation of group work and the usefulness of different
procedures are discussed in "Patterns and Procedures".

What can be learned through small group work.
This is what "A Kind of Learning" is about; group
learning is discussed in relation to the claims of
enthusiasts, research studies and some examples of group
activities.

CONTENTS

The trouble with small groups is that one slips so easily
and sometimes inadvertently into a particular role and
the danger is that in time this becomes the role one
always plays in a group - though the group does not remain
the same.   Every year the students change and what they
do and the purposes for which they meet can change too.
Excellent university teachers do come in many guises
(Sheffield,[1] and Axelrod,[2] describe a variety of
models) and he who is comfortably and unselfconsciously
'being himself' may do very well.   But while no-one can
teach effectively in a style that goes completely against
his grain might it not be profitable for the tutor to
give some thought to the roles he could play in different
kinds of group work?

The small group in university teaching is characterised
by its dual nature.   Its purposes and its work are
intellectual but its nature is social;   interaction
between members of the group at the social level does
affect what can be achieved intellectually.   Small group
teaching is more effective when all members of a group,
tutor and students, recognise this duality, understand
something of the dynamics of the interactions that do
influence their working together and bend these to their
purposes when possible.   Left to themselves a small
group establishes by natural process a modus vivendi that
will allow it to achieve what it can in ways that are
satisfying to most of the group's members.   Part I of
this booklet "What Goes On In Groups" begins with a
description of "The Group As a Group".   It describes the

way a free group achieves a working relationship. We
alert the tutor to the ways in which, for example,
patterns of communication form and to how these can be
used to increase the effectiveness of a seminar or
tutorial. We also point to the difficulties that crop
up as a result of underlying social stresses and suggest
ways of minimising these.

The second section of Part I is "The Individual in the
Group". It discusses how what each student learns,
and the contribution he makes to the learning of others,
in part depends on how well he fits in. As a university
teacher the tutor will, of course, be more concerned
with what the group achieves than with its social relations;
the tutor is responsible for the group's work. But the
tutor is also a member of the group. How well does he
fit in? The third section of Part I, "The Tutor in the
Group", takes the case of the tutor as an unequal member
of any group that is formed for educational purposes;
his authority cannot be put outside the group. Should the
firmness with which he exercises his authority vary with
the kind of work the group is engaged in?

Part II: "Improving Collaboration" is concerned with
the practical ways in which some of the features of
a mature group can be grafted onto a working group which
only meets over a short period of time. A group that
skilfully plays at 'being a group' is likely to work
effectively. Perhaps the most important of these
features is recognition and respect for the rights of
everyone to participate in the group's work. Then
comes willingness to fulfil a special function from
time to time - to take on a role such as gate-keeping.

This means holding the group back so that someone less
forceful than the others is given the opportunity to
contribute.   Gate-keeping is obviously very important
in discussion groups.   Indeed many group management
skills are closely related to the skills needed to
conduct a freely participatory discussion.
("Participatory Discussion" should be read in parallel
with this booklet.)

PART I
WHAT GOES ON IN GROUPS

On the way to each a new tutorial class a lecturer's
mind is probably full of what he means to do with the
class.   But look round as you go in.   What kind of
people are they?   Some individual students stand out,
some do not.   What is <u>this</u> group like?   How will you
get on together?   Each person brings into the group
knowledge, an individual use of language, his own values
and attitudes.

You do look at them as individuals;   try thinking of the
group as an entity.   Freeze them in your mind's eye; is
there a wholeness or pattern in the appearance of the
group, the way they sit and stand and relate to each
other?   Do they look alike, are they similarly accoutred?
Let them talk again;   is there a pattern in their dialogue?
Who speaks to whom in a group, and using whose words, is
important.

A group forms through interaction.   Working together the
same few people acquire a feeling of corporate identity
and various habits and attitudes that are group habits
and not the sum of individual characteristics.   But you
are outside this present group - think of groups you have
belonged to in the past such as people you worked with on
projects, on committees or in workshops.   Were they

1

'groups'? Few university teaching groups ever are in
the special sense we describe, yet the formative processes
of interaction do begin, and small group teaching problems
are often small group behaviour problems. We offer an
account of groups and their behaviour that we hope will be
of practical interest to the university tutor.

1. THE GROUP AS A GROUP

Size

Our concern is with the small group. You will probably
recall groups of anything between 3 and 30. Conventional
wisdom recommends that the effective limits are 6 - 12
with 8 as the magic mean. Fewer than six means a
restriction on activities; larger groups tend to fragment
and reduce the chances of everyone being able to participate.
Larger groups also provide shelter for those who wish to
avoid contact. (Why then use the group method of teaching?)
In large groups the confident and over-talkative dominate
even more than they may do in small groups, and the group
leader also becomes more authoritative.[3,4] For example,
it is only possible to hold anything like a general discussion in a group as large as 30 if the tutor completely
dominates and directs the proceedings.[5]

Setting

Think next of the setting. Special small group teaching
accommodation in universities most often consists of a
room furnished with tables, chairs, a chalkboard, perhaps
a lectern, and few other embellishments. But in some
universities tutors are able to hold seminars and tutorials

in their own rooms. Do you think your own room, filled
with your books and the clutter of your daily living,
provides a better setting? If so, why? If not, why
not? Are the books and clutter friendly or are they
intimidating - are you? Do always ask yourself
the question of how far teaching style should be an
expression of the tutor's personality and how far he
should seek to adapt style and methods to suit particular purposes. Here we ask the same question about
the setting.

Even the point about table/no table is not easily
resolved. Tables are needed if people are going to
write things down or use a map or a model. But if the
group are to discuss what they have been reading on an
equal footing tables may be a barrier to the free
exchange of views. Even the shape of the table may be
important. Abercrombie discusses this point [6]with
reference to the tables specially constructed for the
peace talks between the Americans and the Vietnamese.
Perhaps a setting is only of major significance when a
group first assembles. Then the furnishings and seating
arrangements set the tone. No relationships have been
established; the students are looking for clues. The
head of a table, particularly of a rectangular table, is
unambiguously the dominant position. If the tutor takes
it, then the students' positions are quite clear and
probably much as they were at school. The tutor who
means to take a central role sits at the head of the
table and will be interested to see whether or not the
students resent this in any way. But when the tutor
does not mean to dominate the group too much and avoids
the head of the table the students look for other clues.

3

Is he the only person present with a pile of books in front of him? He is not relinquishing all authority.

What are a group to make of the setting when they enter the room to find no tables and a uniformly-spaced circle of identical chairs? This arrangement has been recommended for participatory discussion groups where the task in hand is something like the analysis of social stratification; students are expected to reveal the attitudes they express in their own lives in order to arrive at a closer understanding of the subject. They certainly feel exposed and if things do not go well there is nothing but the knees opposite to distract them. Nevertheless in a lively group the lack of symbolic divisions may increase participation. [7]

The point is that however you mean to teach do give some thought to how effectively the setting in which you work reinforces or expresses your intentions. And when you begin with clear intentions and create a suitable setting do change it if the intended pattern changes. Suppose, for instance, that you usually begin a group meeting with a mini-lecture from a lectern at the head of the table and student interruptions, questions and contributions break this down into a discussion, would you think of moving away from the head of the table, perhaps walking around a little then sitting down somewhere else, to help keep the discussion open and active? Looking down at your papers and shuffling them should be an effective damper if, on the other hand, you wish to go on with your presentation. Similarly, if you try setting up an open forum with chairs in a circle, lacking the protection of tables, and no-one takes to it

4

do not stay in the circle as you resort to haranguing
the group.   Again get up and walk about.   Try saying
"We are not getting very far like this.   Would you
like me to set the problem of ... more squarely before
you?   I wonder if you have properly appreciated how ...
And next week I would like you all to hand in a short
paper stating your position in relation to the further
problem of ... before we meet.   I shall use these to
analyse your attitudes and will draw a few questions
from them to build on at the meeting."

The time that is left will be used very differently
after an intervention such as that; it may set the
pattern for the next few weeks.   But a change to more
formal and more carefully prepared work may give the
group time to settle down and a switch back to more
open-ended discussion is then on the cards again. Meanwhile, as you set out the orthodox tables and chairs
for next week, do you see yourself sitting at the head
of the table?

Drawing them together

A new group is a collection of individuals.   Each has
his own interests and values, his own use of language and
way of looking at things.   Whatever the nature of the
task a group is to work on, the tutor will be concerned
to draw everyone in.   How successful he is in doing so
may well depend in part on how well he understands how
people behave in groups.   We describe below a pattern
of behaviour based on observation of small groups.   The
tutor's success will also depend in part on his concern
for each individual student; his interest spreads beyond

the likeable, lively or able students.   "The Individual
in the Group" is the next section of this booklet.
There is a related question - is the tutor equally concerned to draw everyone out?   But this depends more
closely on the group's specific objectives and is therefore a question that is raised in "Patterns and Procedures".

A general pattern of behaviour

The presence of the tutor alters the balance of any group.
We wish to depict a pattern of behaviour that is not
complicated by the influence of an externally appointed
leader.   The account that follows is, however, mainly
drawn from a particular study[8] of a further education
group whose observer was their tutor and was therefore
always present.   But he deliberately made few contributions and in no way directed what went on.   This is
a general pattern.   (See Tuckman[9] for a brief analysis
of such records of group behaviour.)   This pattern is
in a sense also the 'free state' to which all kinds of
groups may return when left to themselves.

This group met for 24 two-hour sessions at weekly
intervals, to discuss professional problems they have in
common.   As a group they are therefore distinguished by
their interest in and commitment to the working of the
group.   On the left we describe the stages of development of the group and on the right we sketch the ways
in which an uninterested or apathetic group might
parallel this.   It is the negative aspect of a free
group.

Commitment to the group generates this pattern	Apathy may disrupt the pattern at any point

Stage 1: Appraisal

They are appraising each other: attitudes, background, status, intelligence. They are reluctant to expose themselves; they are wary of involvement, fearing non-acceptance; they are anxious about the inadequacy of their personal knowledge, uncertain as to the method and uneasy at having no-one in authority.

Stage 2: Orientation

The group are forming, seeking the threads that will lead them forward and exploring their inter-actions. They look for roles to play. They begin to express attitudes and opinions and test them out against each other. Accepting the lack of direction they begin to have a care for the shape of their discussion, to look at general principles. When blocked they review issues, cast back, examine what has gone before, find a new way forward.	There is continuing resis-tance to accepting respon-sibility. Discussion is uneven and superficial. There is a lot of sociability. Whenever there is a block discussion founders and there is a show of hostility towards the abdicating authority.

Stage 3: Conflict

There is often open disagreement as attitudes become clearer. Some fundamental differences are exposed, some personal conflicts emerge. Resolution is achieved by emphasis-ing areas of agreement, readiness to go on communicating, by looking for group values that accommodate opposing views.	Conflicts result in the asser-tion of individual positions. The group may fragment. Barriers may be set up against sub-groups or individuals. Some withdraw completely. There is a lot of studied indifference, even aggressiveness.

7

Stage 4: Confidence

Real involvement - they begin to identify with each other's problems, express support without needing to achieve mutual understanding. They work towards understanding and assimilate knowledge through the experience of emotional learning. Participation and interest increase, discussion is freer and wider. New themes emerge. Knowledge comes into the group in response to its felt needs.

Involvement and the discomfort of responsibility for their own learning are evaded. They may insist on dependency on any self-appointed leader, towards whom they express frustrated hostility. They may resist - letting discussion stagnate, missing meetings, sitting at the back, joking, deriding. They may escape by transferring responsibility. If someone is happy to take on the work the rest of the group is happy to let them. In this way two or three friends often take charge.[10]

Stage 5: Control

Group standards emerge through which the group both keeps people in line and shapes the way in which work is handled. They begin to feel a shared identity partly because most people settle into a role within the group, partly because they support and encourage each other. Discussion is disciplined and productive.

They do no parallel independent studying, make few requests for information. They do not become a group. Control remains outside the group.

Stage 6: Termination

If the group goes on meeting for too long it ceases to be productive and is likely to become increasingly introspective, becoming more concerned with group values and esteem than with extraneous subject matter. There is a point at which the group, having achieved what it can in relation to its task, should be disbanded.

First comes appraisal, then orientation followed by a stage
of conflict as real views come out into the open and if
this is resolved a group goes on to confidence and control
before being terminated when its useful life is over. A
tutor will obviously wish to bring his groups to the
confident and controlled stages as quickly as possible.
But teaching groups seldom meet for long enough at a time
nor over a sufficiently long period of time for them to
develop in the way set out above on their own. Groups who
are left completely on their own to build up working
relationships may not achieve this. If a group is to
work together as effectively and as quickly as possible
then the tutor probably has to do two things. One is
to make provision for teaching students something about
group behaviour and the group skills they can practise.
The other is deliberately to graft on to a group some of
the features of mature groups. Possible ways of doing
this are discussed in Part II: "Improving Collaboration".
Meanwhile look at individuals again.

2. THE INDIVIDUAL IN THE GROUP

Being in a group affects both what an individual student
learns himself and the contribution he makes to what
others learn. As a tutor you will be concerned about
the personal and intellectual development of each of your
students; much of what you do and say in seminars or
tutorials may depend on what you observe of the way
students respond to what is going on and on how you interpret their responses. The behaviour of individuals in
groups has been subjected to a great deal of systematic
observation. Here are two charts that summarise a
schedule for such systematic observation.

(i) **The Task Area of Bales" "Interaction process analysis"**

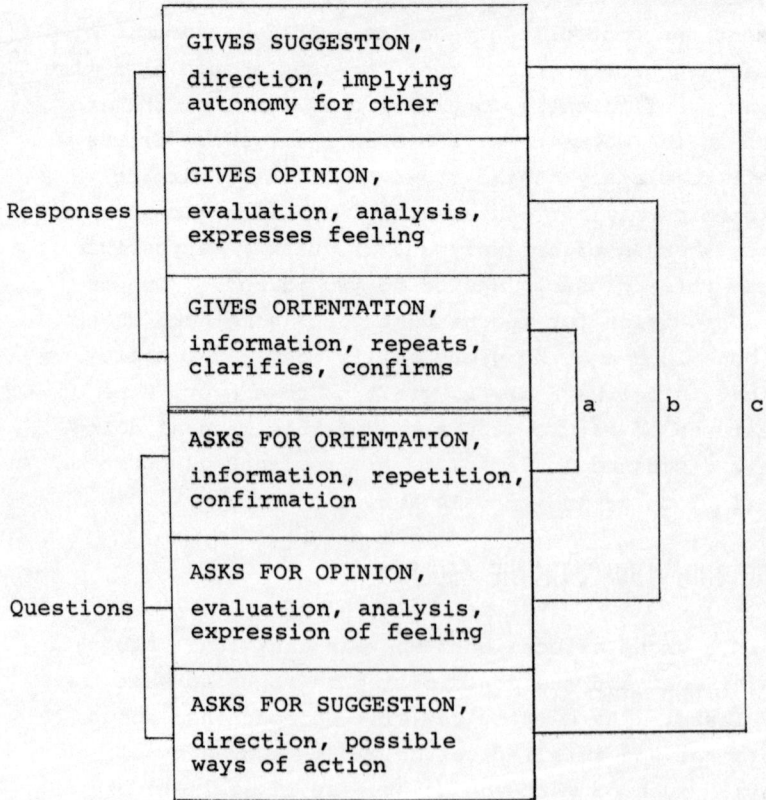

| | | a | b | c |

```
              ┌─────────────────────────────┐
              │ GIVES SUGGESTION,           │
              │ direction, implying         │
              │ autonomy for other          │
              ├─────────────────────────────┤
              │ GIVES OPINION,              │
  Responses   │ evaluation, analysis,       │
              │ expresses feeling           │
              ├─────────────────────────────┤
              │ GIVES ORIENTATION,          │
              │ information, repeats,        │
              │ clarifies, confirms          │
              ╞═════════════════════════════╡   a    b    c
              │ ASKS FOR ORIENTATION,       │
              │ information, repetition,     │
              │ confirmation                 │
              ├─────────────────────────────┤
              │ ASKS FOR OPINION,           │
  Questions   │ evaluation, analysis,        │
              │ expression of feeling        │
              ├─────────────────────────────┤
              │ ASKS FOR SUGGESTION,        │
              │ direction, possible          │
              │ ways of action               │
              └─────────────────────────────┘
```

a = area of communication
b = area of evaluation
c = area of control

(ii)   The Social-emotional Area of Bales' "Interaction
       Process Analysis"

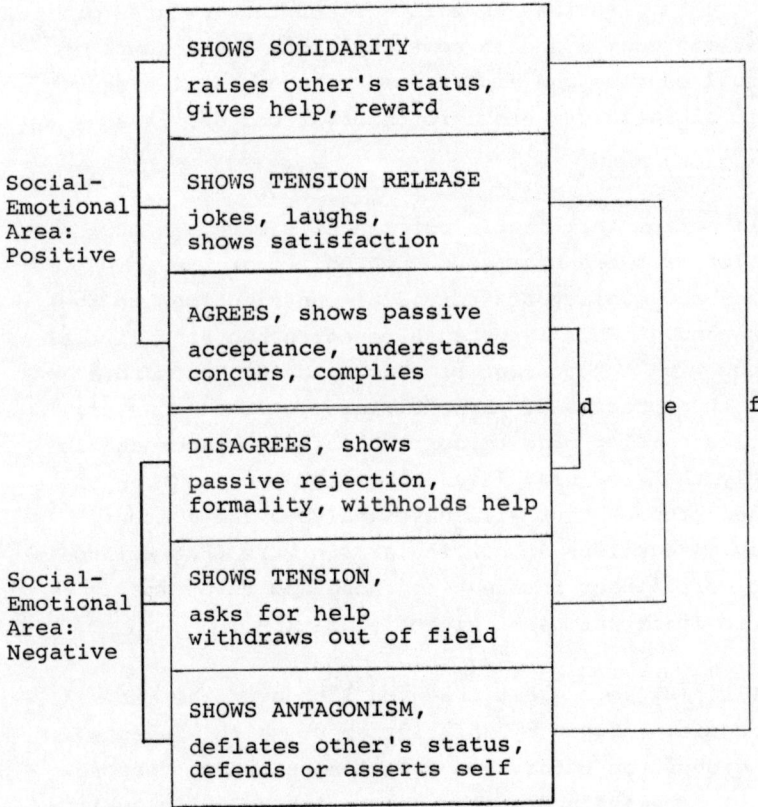

Social- Emotional Area: Positive	**SHOWS SOLIDARITY** raises other's status, gives help, reward
	SHOWS TENSION RELEASE jokes, laughs, shows satisfaction
	AGREES, shows passive acceptance, understands concurs, complies
Social- Emotional Area: Negative	**DISAGREES**, shows passive rejection, formality, withholds help
	SHOWS TENSION, asks for help withdraws out of field
	SHOWS ANTAGONISM, deflates other's status, defends or asserts self

d   e   f

d = area of decision-making
e = area of tension reduction
f = area of group integration

11

These two charts are taken from Bales' book <u>Interaction</u>
<u>Process Analysis</u>.[11] As in all such schedules there is
a theory implicit in the categories he has chosen to use
for analysing group behaviour. This one highlights those
behaviours it describes as being either task-related or
socially expressive and in some ways this makes sense of
the casual conclusions experienced teachers arrive at as
a result of their unsystematic observations of class
behaviour.

You will notice that little reference is made, in our
discussion of these charts,to such points as the
frequency and quality of individual contributions to the
work in hand.   This is because research has been little
concerned with the content of what is said; much more
so with the process of personal interaction. However,
attempts are being made to correct this imbalance and it
is likely that the next five years will see a number of
published studies that will have analysed the content,
of group discussions in particular, in ways that will be
of even more direct interest to those who tutor small
groups in institutions of higher education.

Meanwhile, may we suggest that you look over the two
charts again?   Begin by thinking about which students,
in the groups you tutor, are questioners, which respond.
It is not unrewarding to play about with Bales' classifi-
cations.   You may notice that in your group few ask
questions at all.   Or while most of them ask questions
and offer suggestions from time to time some individuals
stonewall, some always respond by agreeing that that is
a good question, and the well-prepared students may
always give information but never offer solutions to

difficulties or problems.   There may be particular
areas of interpretation that someone avoids.   Why?
Observations of this kind may help you to see students'
individual levels of understanding and provide a thumb-
nail guide to their strengths and weaknesses.

But can you always distinguish between the categories?
How many questions are aggressive?   Come to that, how
many questions are statements?   Is information given
in a fashion that implies non-acceptance of the question,
or dislike of the questioner?   Many apparent requests
for information are attempts to control the group.
Laughter can express hostility, demonstrations of
solidarity can be divisive because sub-groups are forming,
defensive personal expressions may conceal requests for
orientation.   Still, not everyone is prepared to move
out on to this difficult terrain.   It is not to be
expected that many tutors can hope to interpret individual
behaviour with the skill and confidence of those who have
studied and practised the art.   But you can cultivate
awareness of what is happening in the groups you teach.
You can train yourself to pay attention to the way in
which each student is interacting and learning within
the group.   Of all the forms of awareness you can
develop, self-awareness is the most important.

Then how helpful are the students to each other?   There
may be individuals who are quick to move the group in a
particular direction and to question relevance.   This is
all to the good provided this does not provoke resent-
ment.   Contrast this with those who do little but are
always nodding approval of someone else's contributions.
(Remember that in a free group members begin to play

13

special roles and to make distinctive contributions to the group work.) You will notice that another dimension has crept in, that of direction. Towards whom is hostility directed and whose questions are ignored? Who shows exaggerated approval of whose contributions? There may be a private supporters club for a student who is popular and a leader in activities outside the group. Does any one student's contributions seem over-valued by the group as a whole? He may be the 'social star' within the group, the person whom everyone likes to talk to. Networks of communication form within a free group - if your group becomes a lively one you may see something of this. Notice who speaks to whom, who sit together and so forth. If you do spot a 'social star', persuade him of the value of what the group is doing and others may follow, at any rate as long as he retains 'star' status.

Some students freely give their views. There are on the one hand opinion-leaders whose judgment is widely accepted; they are often knowledgeable as well as popular. On the other hand there may be a student who expresses views and even when what he says is a matter of simple fact it may be ignored. Either he himself or his views do not fit easily into the group. People like this may come to see themselves as 'loners', resent it and become disruptive - interrupting and contradicting others. Talkative students sometimes command more attention than the substance of their contributions deserves. And as a corollary when a quiet student gives the solution to a problem the group may seem unaware that he was the author of it. He is not someone they usually notice. One of a tutor's responsibilities may be to guide the group

towards establishing criteria of acceptability that
relate to intellectual rather than social values. It may
be necessary too for the tutor to encourage awareness of
the ever-present tendency to inequality of participation
and to correct any real imbalances.

3. THE TUTOR IN THE GROUP

Small working groups are both social and intellectual in
nature; the tutor too has a double identity. He is
both a member of the group and a figure of authority in
the group. There is no way he can escape this. Suppose
that in accordance with his teaching philosophy he wishes
to be taken for 'just another member of the group'; the
students will not perceive him as being so. (If you
would like to go into this further read the chapters
concerned with 'group-member' leadership in Kemp.)[12]
The tutor is a figure of authority; he has authority, but
he can of course choose the extent to which he wishes to
exercise it directly and he can choose those areas of the
group's activities over which he wishes to exercise direct
control. Before examining these choices let us briefly
consider first the tutor as a member of the group.

Because of his double identity the tutor, as a member of
the group, has to be rather more careful than everyone
else about the values and attitudes he imports into the
group and about the way he behaves. The students are
unlikely to question him in the way they do each other,
or he questions them, and the tutor is not subjected to
the same checks and restraints on his behaviour. Take
values first. As a scholar the tutor is accustomed to
trying to identify his personal bias; as a teacher how

15

scrupulous is he in differentiating between his own
value judgments and his didactic interpretations of his
subject?   Many students are interested in the value
aspects of everything they study;   they seek to relate
what they learn to what troubles them and they are looking
for insights into the possible solutions to world problems.
"Failure to try and deepen understanding, without sacri-
ficing academic aims, undermines the whole theory of the
distinctive value of the tutorial".[13]   Would you agree?

As a tutor you should then give some thought to whether
personal beliefs or ideology infiltrate the group.
Announce them.   We have proposed holding a preliminary
procedural meeting at the start of a course, where the
tutor could contribute a statement of his personal views
of the subject to be studied.   (See page 24.)

Another question to be asked is whether the tutor is bent
on countering views he thinks are being expressed elsewhere.   It has been suggested[14] that seminars can be
a battleground for working out staff rivalries.   Do you
think this is unlikely?   And a final point in relation
to attitudes: the tutor is the authority as well as
being in authority.   But tutors are often called upon
to teach outside their special field and they may be as
reluctant as any student to expose ignorance or uncer-
tainty.   This could be a problem in a discussion group
where the tutor has prepared the ground he thinks it is
desirable to cover and some students try to explore beyond
the limits he has set.   Why not say,"I am not entirely
happy about going any further in this direction, I am
not sure that I have ever properly understood ..." or
"I don't think I am confident about interpreting these

16

plates.   Would anyone like to try working on them and
we could perhaps get X to come in if we get stuck?"
Making things look easy may not encourage the slow
learner; it may be a relief to see that even tutors
have difficulty with some things.

What about behaviour? Tutors talk too much.   (There is
evidence to support this accusation).[15]   And since
tutors are the figures in authority some of the students
will go on smiling and making gratifying responses. Do
take some care and try to develop some kind of objective
self-consciousness! It may not only be a question of
the tutor talking so much that every silence is filled
by his words and what was almost said, by the student who
will not be here next year, is left unsaid for ever.
There may be a breakdown of communication.   The tutor
may be over-forceful in the assertion of the correct (his)
view.   He may be too sharp in cutting off the apparently
irrelevant contribution.   Now not everyone finds small
group work easy; it can be both tedious and painful
sitting there waiting for someone to find their way out
of the maze of their own thoughts or expressions and
wondering whether one should or should not interrupt.
Some tutors are happier with one student at a time. Or
do you always interrupt?   Some tutors are quite unable
to get out of the driving seat.   There are many ways of
teaching, and no one way is best for all circumstances,
but if you are aware of your own tendencies you are in a
better position to modify your behaviour when it is likely
to be counter-productive in a particular teaching situation.
You are also likelier to be ready to devise procedures to
counter your tendencies, even to compensate for your de-
ficiencies! We give an account of discussion skills in
"Participatory Discussion".

Authority

The new tutor may be looking forward to throwing the
pebbles of his hard-won knowledge and insights into the
unknown pools of the students' minds, in a reflective
fashion, to spread ever-widening circles. 'Leadership',
'authority' - these are words that trouble many a
scholar. Authority in the small teaching group has been
discussed most thoughtfully in a paper by Stenhouse,[16]
and the trial publication of A Handbook on Small Group
Teaching and Learning by Rudduck, which reflects
Stenhouse's thinking, adopts the tactful and sensible
approach of inviting its readers to analyse their own
teaching habits in relation to the pertinent questions
the book raises. Material from this trial handbook has
been incorporated in a Nuffield dossier of papers on small
group teaching.[17]   This is essential reading.

Tact is needed because while authority is inescapable and
some teaching is necessarily authoritative the teacher
must not, it is widely thought, become authoritarian.
And while authoritarianism is easily recognised in others
no-one sees it in himself. Or so it is said. What is
the authoritarian tutor like? He decides what the group
are to do, how it will proceed, what will be assessed,
what is relevant, what is acceptable and neither explains
nor discusses decisions with students. He asks questions
that probe and punish. He asks questions to elicit
specific answers. He makes instant judgments on students'
contributions: "Good point", "That's not the point",
"You haven't thought that out". He interprets for other
students. "What you mean by that is ..." The students
always look to him; they usually speak directly to him.

18

They do not pay much attention to each other's contributions; they are trying to find out what is in the tutor's mind. Telling sketch or caricature?

This may serve as a simple cautionary tale for the new tutor; it will probably arouse curiosity in the old hand. The old hand will tell you that "Most of us are, leopard-like, tawny democrats with black spots of authoritarianism." He will tell you about lordlier beasts in the groves of Academe — the glad-to-be-authoritarians and those in democratic sheep's clothing, those who <u>say</u> nothing that is not mild and courteous but are deaf to what they do not want to hear, and the "Co-operate, you swine" brigade whose students always 'freely' choose to do what suits the tutor. Authority can be handled in many ways!

Those who would honestly like to try and see themselves more clearly might like to read about the use of television in the training of teachers. (The analysis of skills and videotaping of performance in the higher education field are reported on by Perlberg.)[18] It might then be possible to take part in a self-confrontation exercise!

Authority may look like a very prickly thistle to the new tutor who had thought that it was the <u>students</u> who were more likely to be aggressive. How is he to cope with it? Perhaps he should begin with a reconsideration of the eternal triangle of teacher, taught and subject. Perhaps the handling of authority is fundamentally a question of respect - respect by teacher and taught for each other and for the subject. Thus the tutor does not

cultivate comfortable relations with the group at the
expense of thoroughness or rigour and he does not pursue
the subject without thought for the students. The tutor
does not assume total and everlasting authority for every
aspect of a group's work. Do you think that the students'
'knowing' will always be subordinate to their tutor's?
The students share in managing the work in hand whenever
both they and their tutor see that they are ready to take
on more responsibility for their own learning. The tutor
recognises that egalitarian form is easier to produce than
its substance; nevertheless he informs the students about
the 'how' and 'why' of his teaching as well as the 'what'
and 'when' and discusses these matters with them if he can.
Authority firmly exercised may order, structure and clarify
what is taught; but the tutor tries to put himself in
each different group's place - what will be the best way
of facilitating their learning?

Authority needs to be defined; a group only works well
when everyone knows where they are in relation to the
tutor.   Stenhouse, [19] among others, warns against authority that comes and goes alarmingly like the Cheshire Cat.
There are times when orderly procedures are the best
means of keeping it in its place. Part II, which follows,
details strategies for improving collaboration. As
you read them think about exactly how you might handle
the tutor's role in each instance and notice how often
this becomes a question of how firmly you are going to
manage the students.

You may be interested in the proposition that tutorial
authority can be expressed in management terms and that
the effectiveness of firm management is related to the

20

kind of situation it controls.[20]   Unambiguously
firm direction will be most effective in two instances.
These are firstly when the task is highly structured
and the tutor gets on well with a group - the operative
phase of a project, the systematic analysis of a text? -
or alternatively where a group of people do not get on
with each other at all and face an ambiguous task.   Here
the tutor might just as well be autocratic.   On the other
hand in intermediate situations less obtrusive management
may enable a group to reach higher levels of performance.
These propositions have yet to be verified by practical
demonstration.   What do you make of them?

PART II
IMPROVING COLLABORATION

Students learn in small groups through co-operative
academic work and it is perhaps precisely the inter-
active element of small group work that brings about
what can be called the higher order types of learning.
By this we mean, for example, the development of
judgment or interpretative skills.   ("A Kind of
Learning" discusses this more fully with several
examples.)   But it is presently within the nature of
things in most universities that few small groups ever
develop a collective personality.   Timetables and
syllabuses militate against their doing so.   The extent
to which group work is directed and controlled by
individual tutors will be a further constraint;   if a
group of students is to find its own best method of
working together they need to assume some of the responsibility for running the group themselves.   And lastly
departmental practice, or the institutional climate may
to some extent dictate the form and procedures of small
group work.   Does this mean that chance will determine
the effectiveness or ineffectiveness of any one group?

We do not think so.   A knowledgeable tutor can do much
to help a group to work effectively together.   Here are
some practical strategies that may create artificially
the working conditions that a confident and controlled

free group develops for itself through inter-action.
It is not to be supposed that each student will find
his group work as satisfying as do the members of a
successful free group, but it is to be expected that
each student may learn more from being part of a group
that skilfully plays at 'being a group' than he might
do otherwise.   What are these strategies?

1. EXCHANGE INFORMATION

Make sure the students know what it is all about.

They should know why they are being taught in this way,
what the precise purposes and objectives of their
particular group are intended to be, what their tasks are,
what they are expected to achieve and how they will be
assessed.   This sort of information could easily be
given as a handout.   Tell them too how this part of
their work relates to what they are taught or are
learning elsewhere on their courses.   Ask them what
they expect from this part of their work.

Teach them how people work in groups.

Direct them to booklets such as this one or circulate
copies for them to read.   If you can find time consider
whether it would be useful to have an informal meeting
to discuss the need for students to learn about and to
demonstrate group skills.   Perhaps you can show them
some film or video-tape that illustrates group teaching
and learning problems and successes.   Perhaps you can
leave them to discuss these amongst themselves.

<u>Hold a preliminary procedural meeting</u>.

If other methods such as handouts have not been used to
spread information here is where you can explain about
the larger aims and specific objectives of the course,
the reasons for using this method, assessment procedures
and so forth.   If it is possible, and if you think it
desirable, consider whether there are areas within which
the students can share in making decisions about the day
to day ordering of the group's work.   This is especially
recommended when it is hoped that group work will achieve
its ends through active participation of the students.
Can they choose the topics to be covered, the tasks
through which they will learn certain skills, the
procedure the group will follow in setting about any
particular kind of task or activity?   The more the
students feel they have had a hand in organising what
goes on the likelier they are to feel concern that it
should go well.

2. ENGINEER CO-OPERATION

<u>Insist on participation</u>.

Well, of course, one cannot do so.   But when participation
is essential you should engineer as much of it as you can.
The extent to which you should feel responsible for doing
so will depend on several factors - your personal inclin-
ation, the nature of the group's tasks or activities,
the experience of the group.   Thus you might feel more
responsible for engineering participation for first year
students than for an honours class.   Clearly some groups
are never going to get beyond the appraisal stage unless

activity is demanded by the way in which the work they
are going to do has been organised.

One can also foster or encourage participation by the
climate that is created inside the group.   We refer
you to the discussion skills in "Participatory Discussion".

Anticipate conflict.

The more a group becomes involved in what it is doing the
more likely it is that conflict (between individuals or
sub-groups) will appear.   Make sure your students
appreciate this point.   Conflict need not necessarily
impede learning but there will be times when the tutor
will have to manage the situation.   Obviously fact and
opinion must be differentiated where they can;   equally
obviously the value systems lying behind declared positions
must be identified.   Harold Laski, a great university
teacher, liked to talk of people shouting at each other
from upper floor windows on different sides of the street -
"arguing from different premises" - as he used to say.
If the conflict arises from misunderstanding let the
origins of the misunderstanding be made clear.   Areas of
agreement should be identified,   the point at which dis-
agreement begins identified and the reasons for the
departure from consensus understood.

Conflict can thus be productive of learning of a very
high quality, provided the tutor has developed the skill
of controlling the tension created.   He seeks to resolve
it through agreement or at least in the agreement to
disagree once the bases of the difference have been
exposed and fully understood.

But conflict may also grow up because communication ceases between adherents of different approaches to a subject; more deeply scored divisions separate them rather than misunderstandings.   Thus a 'star' in the group may feel strongly about examining historical causes in depth.   He normally takes a large share of the discussion; he and three or four others of like mind begin to dominate the proceedings.   One or two other students mean to look for explanations of events within the widest possible context of contemporary circumstances.   They have to fight to get a word in.   Now the tutor may well leave things alone if the historical causes group are developing the subject in line with syllabus requirements; from time to time he will make space for occasional 'wider context' points to be made.   But if the dominant few are diverging from the essential pattern of the group's work it may become necessary for the tutor to intervene firmly or to change the structure and procedures within which they are working.   Sub-groups can be used.   (See below.)   The tutor looks out for means of improving the goodness of fit between the communication pattern within the group and the layout of its task.

In the rare instances when friction comes from strong personal hostilities or a collision of prejudices it may be worthwhile trying to sort this out outside formal teaching hours.

Use Sub-Groups.

If sub-groups form in opposition to each other involve them in preparing alternative position papers on a theme. Or if the effect of one increasingly dominant sub-group

is judged to be no longer productive the members could be
dispersed among syndicates.   The syndicate method is a
form of small group work that engages smaller groups,
called syndicates, on a collective piece of work of their
own which they organise for themselves and then present
to the whole group when they have made something of it.
The presence of members of a strong social sub-group in
different syndicates might make for more interested and
livelier discussion of each syndicate's presentation to
the whole group.   (See Collier,[21] for a description
of syndicates at work.)   When you come to consider
the possible use of new forms of group work as suggested
both here and in "Patterns and Procedures", you must make
a thorough survey of the practical difficulties involved
and the time at your disposal.   Obviously we feel they
are worthwhile suggestions but if they are adopted too
hastily or without proper preparation the results may not
be what you expect.   Similarly, bear in mind that what
are sensible suggestions for experienced groups may not
be so for first year students.

Encourage any moves to assume responsibility for their own learning.

A successful group will want to begin to influence the
direction of its activities.   You can acknowledge this
by suggesting that they begin by sharing in the choice,
say, of tasks or of topics for discussion right at the
start.   Any further moves they then begin to make themselves in this direction should be encouraged - within
reason.   The caveat has to be made because the tutor is
responsible for ensuring that the essential points in the
syllabus are covered.   Finding a balance between

speculative exploration of the peripheral and systematic
coverage of the essentials is not easy (Watt,[22]
discusses this more fully).   One has to learn how to
edge even the most strong-headed group back to the
central issues designated by the syllabus.   Similarly
a good group may establish their own standards; if the
tutor requires higher but still realistic standards he
may have to intervene.

But you will find that some groups, or some students,
are reluctant to accept any measure of responsibility
for their own learning.   They groan and grumble whenever they are asked to resolve issues for themselves,
or are denied handouts.   Again the tutor will try to
edge them over towards undertaking to do just a little
more and a little more and the group should be ready to
tolerate the discomfiture this may provoke. Assessment
can be both carrot and stick.   More frequent but
shorter assignments may get them going.   Or can you
change the form of assessment?   This group might enjoy
small projects.

3. PLAYING ROLES

People play roles in real life.   And in a free small
group the members take on roles vis à vis the others;
individuals gradually assume a specific function that
suits their personality and their relationship to the
rest of the group.   Thus one becomes the organiser,
another the expert on what has gone before, another is
the person who always smoothes over disagreements.
There is not going to be time for everyone naturally

to find their place and their part to play in a teaching
group.   But observation has led to the description of
certain roles that must be filled if the group is to
function efficiently.   Once everyone recognises this
and is prepared to accept some of the responsibility
for what goes on, then they can be ready to take on one
of these roles whenever it is necessary.   In other words
there are certain roles to be played from time to time -
a simple example is time-keeping.   Anyone can take it
on, no-one plays at it all the time since it is unlikely
to be their natural role, and because someone does take
it on the group gets through what it wishes to cover.

Variation in the roles people play fits in with wider
educational purposes.   One does not want everyone just
to go on getting better at what they do well.   It is,
however, far from easy for anyone to re-adjust ways of
using language and of behaving that have been shaped
elsewhere.   Role-playing allows people to practise
making this kind of adjustment in a way that does not
threaten their personal security.   It can be seen to
be a special skill.

Clearly, if too much is made of it, or it becomes a
formal charade, then role-playing could be a farce.
But, while it may seem artificial and slightly silly to
some, it does require the exercise of restraint and self-
discipline and can contribute a great deal to the smooth
functioning of a group.   The list of roles that follows
is in a sense the naming of skills to practise.   We have
taken our examples from Hill[23] and Klein.[24]

<u>Roles that are to do with responsibility for what is</u>
<u>going on in a group</u>. (If there is a formal leader these
are leadership roles.)
Someone who does the

Gate-keeping:	making sure that everyone who wishes to do so has an opportunity to speak, letting people in to speak.
Time-keeping:	checking on the order of proceedings.
Watching relevance:	"What does that relate to?" "We have all been saying ... where does what you say take us?"
Initiating:	starting things off, bringing in new topics.
Terminating:	summarising, or just expressing the group's arrival at the end of something.

Those are all neutral chairmanship roles.   Here are a
few more complex functions.   Someone, other than the
leader, can do the

Co-ordinating:	formulating proposals or solutions, reconciling opposite views, probing possible developments.
Organising:	there is often need for someone to keep in mind the true nature of the task, and to open up the question of what steps should be taken in what order.
Facilitating:	someone is needed to ease discussion. He often sees what is relevant, asks for substantiating information,

points to connections. He is
interested in what others say and
often links contributions to one
another, creating opportunties
for others to speak. He discourages
irrelevancies. He may pad the
discussion a bit when others are
slow to respond.

Roles that are to do with the academic task in hand.
(If a group is sufficiently mature these are roles the
tutor leaves to students.)

Interpreters: they explain what people mean in
other words. They try to clarify
what people say and show how it
relates to what has gone before.

Evaluators: they approve or disapprove of what
the others contribute. They
remark on the acuteness, relevance,
sense, of what is said.

Critics: these are a higher form of evaluator.
They question as well as interpreting and evaluating. Their
judgment is usually respected.

Experts: these are resource persons, founts
of knowledge, suppliers of information. They add to what others
say and answer questions.

<u>Roles that are to do with group morale and effective</u>
<u>working together</u>.   (Everyone should take up these
roles from time to time.)

Facilitators:	this role comes in again here.
Listeners:	they pay attention when others speak, demonstrate acceptance of other contributions, look at the speaker.
Morale-builders:	they make encouraging remarks, and respond in a positive way to others' contributions. They have a friendly manner towards everyone and are expressive and sociable.

Role-playing is a cultivated response to the needs of
the group and not to a person's inner needs. Nevertheless there is always an underlying tendency for a group
to revert to the 'free state' of that phase of development pattern, described on pages 7 and 8, to which
they now approximate. Individuals (including the
tutor) will edge over into roles that satisfy them
whether or not this is what suits the group's work.
One hopes one will not meet many groups where everyone
is contending to have their needs met! But you will
have to expect to lose a few. Would you then revert to
more tightly structured procedures?

4. CONTROLLED INFORMALITY

Students with limited experience of intensively intellectual group work may feel rejected and uncomfortable if

ways are not found of inviting their participation.
They may need to begin by expressing something of themselves and talking to the others about what they think
and what their experience has been.   Without this they
may not feel that they can contribute.   If no-one
understands who they are will anyone properly understand
what they say, or what they are trying to say?   A
research study[25] reports that about 30% of students'
thoughts during small group discussions were about themselves and other persons.   It is not easy to reduce
this personal element, especially in discussion classes.
It is usually less of a problem when the small group
work is an integral part of the course rather than
being simply appended to lectures.

One way of initiating more disciplined habits is to give
time specifically for less formal chat.   Perhaps an
introductory free-for-all can serve both as a warming-
up exercise and a welcome.   Invite the students to talk
about 'what they really think'.   A skilful tutor will
move easily from this warming-up phase into the proper
academic work of the group.   The transition need be
marked by no more than a pause, a change of tone, a
greater deliberation;   there will not be a sudden icing
over of the atmosphere as the group settles down to work.
Alternatively the tutor might say at the very first
meeting "I think it would be profitable to spend the
first five minutes every week in going over what we have
been doing and what we are going to do", and the tutor
then establishes that this is the part of the meeting
where informality is the rule.   The point is to make
these periods quite distinct;   for the rest of the time
work goes forward in serious academic style and remarks

like "People in Huddersfield simply don't think this is
of any importance at all!" are met by "Well, tell us
what they do think at the beginning of next week's
tutorial."

First year students may find it most difficult to engage
in disciplined discussion that eschews all personal
expressions of opinion, especially when a subject is
completely new to them. In feeling their way around a
subject people try to connect it to what they already
know and this may mean to personal experience. Should
they begin with informal discussion that allows them to
bring in a lot of personal opinion? Hill[23] has
worked out a formal method of organising group discussion
that takes the students step by step through the systematic
analysis, or review, of a topic and, by restricting contributions to what is proper to each step at each step,
the method prevents students from expressing personal
opinions until they have completed the analysis. This
method has been widely taken up and may be especially
useful with first year classes. Experience suggests that
a final interchange of opinions is then a fruitful one.
We offer the Hill method as one of our patterns in
"Patterns and Procedures", it is summarised in more
detail there, but if you are really interested Hill's own
booklet "Learning Thru Discussion" provides a full and
lively practical exposition of the method and the
thinking behind it.

A second strategy is to encourage some informality, but
not too much, while the group are at work. At the same
time the tutor tries to foster awareness of the distinc-
tion between using personal exchanges, both to make it

possible to work together in the first place and to make
it easier at all times, and supposing that personal
exchanges of opinion constitute a serious discussion. It
becomes easier with experience. It is all a question of
balance; if a group is not to be too rigidly intellectual
all the time neither is it to become a personal free-for-
all. Balance is achieved through control, who is to
exercise the control? In a free group everyone really
gets to know everyone else, balances are worked out.
Such a group can control itself. Personal self-expression
that the group thinks inappropriate will be met either with
open condemnation or by no-one responding. On the other
hand think of a class who have been accustomed to firm
control by their teacher. Leave them to work on their
own and there will be outbreaks of horse-play, noisiness,
constant joking, irregular attendance. When they do get
down to work they will probably have to contend with bad
habits such as not properly listening to each other, too
much chattiness and streams of personal analogies and
allusions.

The tutor necessarily decides how firm he needs to be to
begin with. It is widely accepted that some sociability
is needed in a working group. One hears of seminars
where the students have never talked to each other at all
and where only two or three of a group of ten ever partici-
pated in the seminar unless specifically requested to do so.
Surely these are exceptional cases? Sociability is needed
when people meet to learn together for obvious reasons.
Learning involves moving away from the security of what is
known into the unknown; it implies change; it re-introduces
the possibility of failure. In a friendly group all this
is possible without anyone's self-esteem being damaged too

much by mistakes. If a group does reach a stage where
students admit confusion, struggle to overcome miscon-
ceptions and declare what they do think then they may
well reach out further - if they can keep the temperature
of the group both warm enough and cool enough. They can
only do this where there is a working relationship and
relationships are built through social interaction.

Some sociability may be necessary but how much? The
precise nature of the group's work will be one determining
factor. Clearly if everyone is individually working out
problems, or they are building a model together or the
tutor is actively teaching for most of the session -
explaining, expounding and demonstrating - there will be
a built-in level of informality. And in any case one
need not bother too much about creating a deliberately
open atmosphere. Whereas if the students need to thrash
out the energy relationships in a metabolic system that
is commonly misunderstood, or the relation of events to
the development of political theories, then the whole
exercise may be abortive if no-one says what they think.
Another factor that is always to be taken into account is
the group's experience. If they have never taken part
in informal collaborative work they may need both
direction and encouragement.

PART III

LAST WORDS

1. THERE IS NO LAST WORD

You may disagree vehemently with the bias of this booklet
and deny the practicality of everything it recommends.
Nevertheless we would like to think that if you have read
it your perception of your students and their tutor will
have changed a little.   You will have looked at them as
people in a group.   Perhaps how you look at them is
less important than the fact of looking in the first place.

It is sometimes postulated that the value of any preparation for teaching, of training courses or an individual's
own homework, lies in the focussing of attention!

2. BUT WE SHOULD LIKE TO SAY ...

That if there is to be co-operative work in a group
and the fostering of learning in each member of it then
some attention must be paid to each person as a person.
In academic terms contributions will always be unequal.
It has been said that students have to be socially
assertive to participate in situations where they are
intellectually inferior.[26]   But the socially assertive
are as likely to inhibit active learning by their fellows
as are the intellectually more able.   If the fostering

of individual learning is a major purpose of small group
work, and not just the formal one, then a shift has to
be made towards valuing someone's contribution in
relation to his own prior achievement. The group will
set a proper value on honest attempts to overcome hurdles
and will reward, by approval, every step their fellow
student takes towards mastery of concepts and the
expression of his own understanding.

While the competitive spirit prevails the greatest
impediment to free speaking may be the fear of exposing
ignorance and conceptual confusion in front of one's
fellows - far more than in front of the tutor.[27] No
new procedures nor forms of assessment can counter this.

For some students it may be that, for a time, the tutorial
or seminar group is the only significant group to which
they belong. The group as a whole, or individuals within
it, may be the only mirror which gives the student an
image of himself. The social values of small groups are
important; they are educational values. One can make
these values clearer without being damned as an apostle
of manic informality.

Many tutors begin each course with a casual 'get-together' -
perhaps coffee in the seminar room. They hope to start
each group along the way towards discovering an identity
of its own.[28] At these meetings they make sure that
each student becomes known - in the sense that something
of his background, interests and aspirations is disclosed
to the others present. When it is possible to encourage
other minor social activities that might accelerate the
process of group formation, do help - provided that you

do not see yourself as a missionary. There will be
little response to attempts to mount a programme for
the staff in your department to get to know their
students better. Both staff and students are pressed
to make the best use of their time. 'Do-gooding'
activities will be just another distraction. In their
daily commerce both staff and students, more often than
not, ignore signals that do not bear on their narrow,
short-term, joint concerns. Communication remains
direct and simple. [29]

Still, here are your small number of students. Snyder[29]
points to the possibility of providing for more legitimate
encounters. Are there opportunities for undergraduates
to work for a time as assistants in your laboratory,
your offices or on your field-work? Can they help with
extra-mural teaching? Can they act as demonstrators in
practical classes or as 'proctors'[30] in self-
instructional systems? An excellent illustration of
how, for example, off-campus field-work can affect staff
and student perceptions of one another is "Both Ends of
a Log".[31] The Nuffield Foundation have also
published[32] a stimulating discussion document that is
a study of the students' experience of academic life and
underlines our main point. Working relationships must
be created if learning in small groups is to be effective.

39

SUGGESTIONS FOR FURTHER READING

If you would like to read more about the topics and issues we have introduced we recommend the following books and articles. We have already referred to several of them in the text.

GROUP PROCESS AND STRUCTURE

KLEIN, J. (1966) *Working with Groups*.
London, Hutchinson.

A major source for this booklet.

OTTAWAY, A.K.C. (1966) *Learning Through Group Experience*.
London, Routledge & Kegan Paul.

Gives a detailed account of how patterns of behaviour develop in small groups.

DAVIS, J.H. (1969) *Group Performance*.
Reading, Mass., Addison-Wesley.

Provides an easy to read introduction to topics such as how individual performance compares with group performance in respect of different kinds of task.
Much of this is relevant to teaching.

KEMP, G.C. (1964) *Perspectives on the Group Process*.
Boston, Mass., Houghton Mifflin.

Is edited to provide a coherent inter-disciplinary survey of research and opinion on such topics as group patterns, group self-evaluation, and how groups respond to different styles of leadership. The book broadly distinguishes group-centred, democratic and authoritarian types in a way that is useful to the teacher. Though quoting the most reputable of authorities this book is easy for the layman to read and would sensibly lead on to more rigorous treatments.

There are two good collations of extracts from studies and reviews of research in the small group field and from the authors of currently respected theories. Both are worth browsing through.

CARTWRIGHT, D. & ZANDER, A. (Eds.) (1968) *Group Dynamics: Research and Theory*.   London, Tavistock.

SMITH, P.B. (Ed.) (1970) *Group Processes*.
Harmondsworth, Penguin.

SYSTEMATIC OBSERVATION OF BEHAVIOUR IN GROUPS

Research suggests that trainee school teachers, taught to use a
categorical observation schedule, do become far more conscious of
how they themselves behave and of how they could, say, respond to
pupils in ways other than those they use habitually.   Flanders is
the analyst of classroom behaviour whose schedules are most popular.

> FLANDERS, N.A. (1970) *Analysing Teaching Behaviour*
> Reading, Mass., Addison-Wesley.
>
> You may find this simplistic and too precise in its analyses
> of behaviour.   But for anyone interested in this approach,
> Flanders is necessary reading.

INTERPERSONAL COMMUNICATION

> The many facets of person-to-person communication, both
> verbal and non-verbal, as they are presently described and
> understood are thoroughly explored in both
>
> ARGYLE, M. (1967) *The Psychology of Interpersonal Behaviour*
> Harmondsworth, Penguin
>
> LAVER, J. & HUTCHESON, S. (Eds.) (1972) *Communication in
> Face to Face Interaction.*
> Harmondsworth, Penguin.

TEACHING AND LEARNING IN THE SMALL GROUP

> ABERCROMBIE, M.L.J. (1974) *Aims and Techniques of Group Teaching.*
> (3rd Edition). London, S.R.H.E.
>
> The authoritative work.
>
>
> NUFFIELD GROUP for Research and Innovation in Higher Education,
> in collaboration with RUDDUCK, J. (1976) *Small Group Teaching.*
> London.   Nuffield Foundation.
>
>
> RICHARDSON, E. (1967). *Group Study for Teaching.*
> London, Routledge & Kegan Paul.
>
> Gives a perceptive account of non-directive tutoring.
> She is good on the effects of a group's setting and general
> ambience, and on the way in which methods of assessment have
> far-reaching effects on a group's work.
>
> STENHOUSE, L. (1972) "Teaching Through Small Group Discussion:
> Formality, Rules and Authority."
> *Cambridge Journal of Education 2:* pp. 18-24.
>
> This is essential reading for the new tutor.

REFERENCES

1. SHEFFIELD, E.F. (Ed.) (1974). *Teaching in the Universities: No One Way.*
   Montreal. McGill - Queen's University Press.
2. AXELROD, J. (1973). *The University Teacher as Artist*
   San Francisco. Jossey-Bass.
3. McFARLAND, H.S.N. (1962). "Education by Tutorial".
   Universities Review, 34: pp.45-51.
4. BENNE, K.D. & LEVIT, G. (1953). "The nature of groups and helping groups improve their operation".
   Review of Educational Research, 23(4), pp.289-308.
5. COTSONAS, N.T. et al. (1958). "Adapting the group discussion technique for use in large classes".
   Journal of Medical Education, 33: pp.152-162.
6. ABERCROMBIE, M.L.J. (1974). *Aims and Techniques of Group Teaching.*
   (3rd edition). London. S.R.H.E.
7. RICHARDSON, E. (1967). *Group Study for Teaching.*
   London. Routledge & Kegan Paul.
8. OTTAWAY, A.K.C. (1966). *Learning Through Group Experience.*
   London. Routledge.
9. TUCKMAN, B.W. (1970). In SMITH, P.B. (ed) *Group Processes.*
   Harmondsworth, Penguin.
10. BION, W.R. (1948-51). *Experience in Groups.*
    Human Relations, I-IV.
11. BALES, R.F. (1951). *Interaction Process Analysis.*
    Cambridge, Mass. Addison-Wesley.
12. KEMP, C.G. (ed) (1964). *Perspectives on the Group Process.*
    Boston. Houghton Mifflin.
13. McFARLAND, H.S.N. (1962). *Op.cit. (see 3 above)*
14. WATT, I. (1964). "The Seminar"
    Universities Quarterly, 18: pp.369-389.
15. POWELL, J.P. (1974). "Small group teaching methods in higher education".
    Educational Research, 16(3): pp.163-171.
16. STENHOUSE, L. (1972). "Teaching through small group discussion: formality, rules and authority".
    Cambridge Journal of Education, 2: pp.18-24.
17. RUDDUCK, J. (1974). *Small Group Teaching and Learning, Handbook II (Trial Edition).*
    Norwich. University of East Anglia, U.G.C. Small Group Teaching Project.
    Material from this trial edition has now been incorporated in *Small Group Teaching.* London. The Nuffield Foundation (1976).
18. PERLBERG, A. (1975). "When Professors confront themselves".
    Paper presented at the International Conference on 'Improving University Teaching', Heidelberg, 9-11 May, 1975.
19. STENHOUSE, L. (1962). *Op.cit. (see 16 above)*
20. FIEDLER, F.E. (1970). In SMITH, P.B. (ed.) *Group Processes.*
    Harmondsworth. Penguin.

21. COLLIER, K.G. (1966). "An experiment in University teaching". *Universities Quarterly, 20:* pp.336-348.
22. WATT, I. (1964). *Op.cit. (see 14 above)*
23. HILL, W.F. (1969). *Learning Thru Discussion.* London. Sage Publications.
24. KLEIN, J. (1966). *Working with Groups.* London. Hutchinson.
25. BLOOM, B.S. (1954). "The thought process of students in discussion". In FRENCH, S.J. (ed.) *Accent on Teaching.* New York. Harper.
26. MARRIS, P. (1965). *The Experience of Education.* London. Routledge & Kegan Paul.
27. PARLETT, M. (1969). "Undergraduate teaching observed". *Nature, 223:* pp.1102-4.
28. ABERCROMBIE, M.L.J. (1974). *Op.cit. (see 6 above)*
29. SNYDER, B.R. (1971). *The Hidden Curriculum.* New York. Knopf.
30. KELLER, F.S. (1968). "Goodbye Teacher...". *Journal of Applied Behavioural Analysis, 1:* pp.78-89.
31. "Both Ends of a Log" (1975). Film produced by the Film Centre, Tertiary Education Research Centre, University of New South Wales, Kennington, New South Wales, Australia.
32. PARLETT, M., SIMONS, H. et al. (1976). *Learning from Learners.* London. The Nuffield Foundation.